GETTING STARTED ON GARDEN DESIGN

What do we mean when we talk about designing a garden? For most of us, after all, making a garden is an incremental process.

Much of it we inherit on moving day, whether it's a manicured lawn and well-tended border; a neglected, overgrown tangle in need of a machete and lots of loving care; or the dauntingly barren canvas of an empty builder's lot surrounding a brand-new suburban home.

And much of a garden evolves over time. We dig new flower beds and enlarge old ones; cut down dying trees and plant young saplings; build a deck, lay a patio, excavate a pond or replace the fence.

Whether you're designing a new landscape from scratch, renovating an established one or merely adding a few new features, garden design is about the way you live, the things you like to do and the plants you love to grow.

This book will focus your garden design thoughts on your particular needs, on what you have to work with and how you're going to use your garden. We'll show you how to develop a plan that will work for you and, along the way, you'll learn about the practical and horticultural considerations of gardens and their plants.

By bringing together the principles of good design with the practical necessities, you can create the garden of your dreams.

CONSIDERING YOUR NEEDS

Before you make any design decisions, put your thinking cap on and consider how you want your garden to work for you and your family.

You'll want to think about:

- how the garden will be used
- what the style of the garden should be
- how much time will be devoted to creating the garden and its upkeep
- the kinds of plants you like
- how to create a focal point
- the colours you like in a garden
- the effect of sun and shade on your use of the garden and the plants you can grow
- whether you need to hide an unsightly view or highlight a beautiful view
- the look of the garden in spring, summer, fall and winter
- how long you plan to live in your home

DESIGNING FOR DINING

- A garden dining area should be close to the kitchen to facilitate carrying dishes, linens and food in and out.

- To add to the ambiance of al fresco dining after dark, plant fragrant, white flowers that shimmer in the dark and waft their scent in the breeze. Try daphne, alba roses, mock orange, Nicotiana alata, Oriental lilies and summersweet (Clethra).

- Outdoor speakers can provide music with dinner; a small tinkling fountain gives a different kind of background.

- Add a potting cupboard nearby; not only will it hold essential tools, pots and bags of soil, it can double as a dining sideboard.

Comfortable outdoor furniture on the patio brings the dining room into the garden.

HOW WILL YOU USE YOUR GARDEN?

It can help to think of the way or ways you want to use your garden if you think of the garden like rooms in a house.

If the front yard is the "foyer," then the back can be metaphorically divided into living room (with comfy seating), dining room (with barbecue and outdoor table and chairs), playroom (swing set, croquet field, basketball court), pantry (veggie patch and herb garden) and utility room (lawn mower and tools).

The walls along the property line might be a leafy hedge or fence, but the divisions between the garden rooms themselves could be shrubs, trellis screens or even island beds.

The floor could be a plush carpet of green lawn, easy-care paving or wooden decking. The halls are the walkways and paths.

And decor? That's the furniture and all those great plants!

DESIGNING FOR KIDS

If you have young children, you might want a magical garden where they can build sandcastles, play hide-and-seek, weave daisy chains and survey the world from their very own treehouse.

• Design a flower bed for children in a sunny spot with good soil where they can try their hand growing plants from seed. Choose sure-to-germinate plants like marigold, zinnia, sunflower, nasturtium, tomato, pumpkin and beans.

• Help little ones make a bean teepee. Plant runner bean seeds at the base of three or four bamboo stakes that have been pushed into the soil in a circle. Leave a space for the entrance then tie the stakes at the top with twine. By mid-summer, the teepee will be a leafy "hideout."

Play equipment is positioned so it can be seen from the house yet the lawn acts as a buffer between play area and patio.

The welcoming red front door is echoed by the cheerful reds in the flower beds.

GOOD GARDEN BONS

I t's important to understand that every good design begins with a permanent framework — the garden bones as they're called. Good bones are the foundation on which the ultimate success of your garden depends.

These are built features such as walkways, walls and patios. They're also the living bones — the deciduous and evergreen trees and shrubs that form the upper canopy in your garden and give it interest all year long. (Our companion book in this series, *Plantings*, can help you develop a strategy for building the living bones in your garden.)

Nothing can substitute for the bones of a stately tree. Its leaves offer cool, dappled shade; its blossoms, ephemeral beauty and its sturdy trunk symbolizes all that's strong and right in a garden. Bark, blossoms, leaves, fruit and berries — trees play an essential role in every successful design.

DESIGN TIPS

Once you've made your initial wish list, gather as many great design ideas as you can.

- Read gardening magazines and books.
- Join a garden club.
- Sign up for an evening design course.
- Walk the streets in your neighbourhood, making note of your favourite gardens and what you like about them.
- Go on garden tours (and be sure to take your camera!).

Shrubs like forsythia and permanent features like the bird bath are the "bones" that bring a sense of structure to this garden all year.

Developing a Plan

I n the same way that a builder can't proceed without the architect's plans, a garden can't be comprehensively designed or even modified before there's a drawing on paper. In design language, this is known as a "site plan."

MAKING A SITE PLAN

You need a site plan to start the garden design process but your plan doesn't have to be complicated. All you need are a measuring tape, pencil, graph paper and a means of converting big measurements to small ones (calculating a scale, in other words). A designer's ruler is marked off in equivalent scales; one inch on paper, for example, might equal ten feet on the ground. Don't worry too much about scale, though. Just try to sketch all of your yard (property line, house, garage, walkways, patio and/or deck and flower beds) on paper in approximately the same proportions they are in their full size.

If there are big trees in adjacent yards, draw those in, too, since their roots and the shadows they cast may affect your garden. And be sure to record which areas of your property are in sun and shade, whether there is a slope that might affect usage and if there are raised or damp areas.

Once you have your site plan drawn, make several copies of it and use each one to sketch in a different design scheme. Or lay transparent paper over the top and do rough sketches of the changes you want to make around the elements that will remain fixed — the house, fence, large trees and so on.

PLAN A DESIGN

Don't overlook another great design tool: your camera. What would the front yard look like with the old sidewalk gone and a new one sweeping from the driveway to the front door? Would a deck suit the back of the house?

Take some photos of your property or areas you're thinking of changing. Enlarge the resulting prints, make lots of photocopies, then sketch in that new walk or deck right on the photocopy. The facing page shows an example of this technique; the next two pages show some creative design possibilities for this front yard.

DESIGN CONCEPTS

These concepts for the house on page 9 illustrate two very different garden styles. On this page, a formal garden has been designed. It is characterized by the straight walkway leading from the sidewalk, built from square cut flagstone, and the formal banding that articulates the access off the driveway. The banding is further defined by a low boxwood hedge. Overall, the look is very controlled and precise. The facing page shows a casual or cottage-y interpretation of the same space. Shapes are less rigidly defined and the walkway, made from randomly cut flagstone, curves up to the house. The curved planting beds and the loose and somewhat sprawling plants contribute to the relaxed feel of this design.

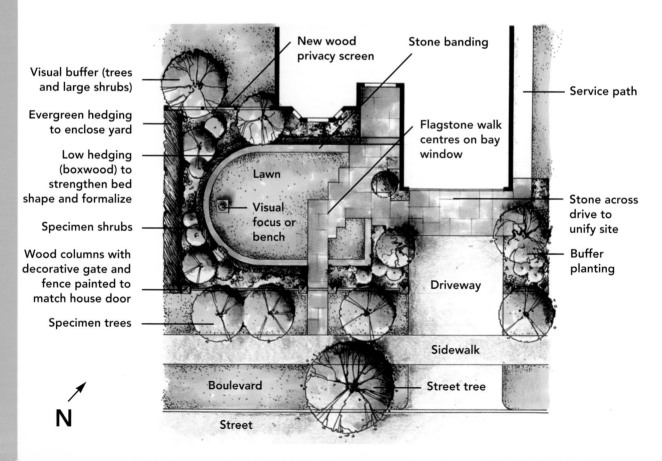

Visual buffer (trees and large shrubs)

Evergreen hedging to enclose yard

Low hedging (boxwood) to strengthen bed shape and formalize

Specimen shrubs

Wood columns with decorative gate and fence painted to match house door

Specimen trees

New wood privacy screen

Stone banding

Flagstone walk centres on bay window

Lawn

Visual focus or bench

Service path

Stone across drive to unify site

Buffer planting

Driveway

Sidewalk

Street tree

Boulevard

Street

N

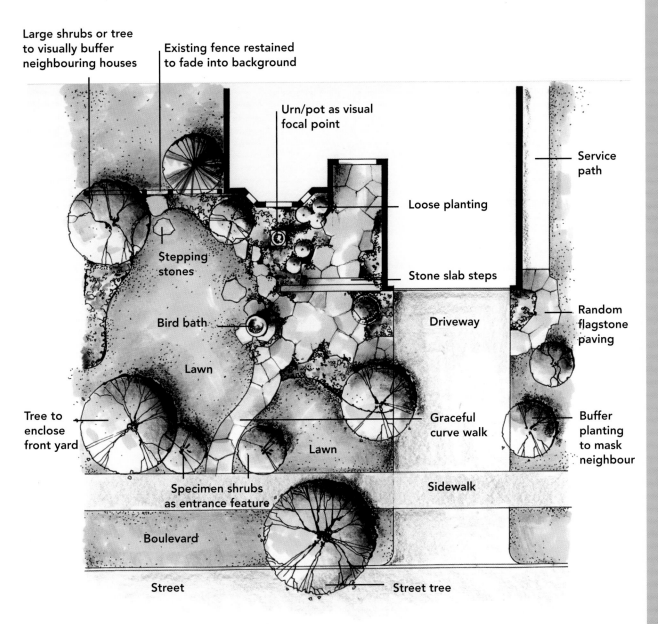

Large shrubs or tree to visually buffer neighbouring houses

Existing fence restained to fade into background

Urn/pot as visual focal point

Service path

Loose planting

Stepping stones

Stone slab steps

Bird bath

Driveway

Random flagstone paving

Lawn

Tree to enclose front yard

Graceful curve walk

Lawn

Buffer planting to mask neighbour

Specimen shrubs as entrance feature

Sidewalk

Boulevard

Street

Street tree

N

WORKING TOWARD A DESIGN

As you work with your finished site plan to develop a design, certain natural variables will guide your hand. These are:

- light (the amount of sun or shade)
- flat areas and slopes of your property (its topography)
- soil (rich or poor, sandy or clay, acid or alkaline)

Other factors to be considered relate to your property:

- its size and shape (square, rectangular, pie-shaped, narrow, tiny, large)
- elements of scale and proportion in your yard and the house
- views (good or bad in your garden or outside your garden)

The following pages will help you to focus on these details. Once you've read through them, you may want to, or need to, revisit your site plan to make changes that are important in view of your garden and how you plan to use it.

Then, it's on to the fun stuff: all the elements of garden design that make the garden your own!

DESIGN TIP

The more time spent planning, the more time, frustration and money you'll save later.

An inviting corner has been created where one can sit and admire the view of the garden.

LIGHT

Much of the success of your garden design depends on knowing where the sun and shade fall at different times of the day and different times of the year. It's not just important for your plants, which have particular growing requirements for sun or shade, but for you, too. The patio that's lovely in the early morning sun can feel like an oven by about 4 p.m. on a July day if it doesn't receive some shade.

To understand where light falls in your garden, watch the path of the sun and see where shadows are created. Ideally, you'll do this over the course of a summer, but you can make do with just one day of observation. If your garden receives full sun for 75% of daylight hours including between 11 a.m. and 2 p.m., with full southern exposure, you have a sunny location. A partially shaded location receives early morning sun (until 11 a.m.) or late afternoon sun (after 2 p.m.). Full shade is considered to be an area that receives a maximum of 2 or 3 hours of sun in the early morning or after 4 p.m.

You can accommodate too much sun or too much shade with good design and carefully selected plants.

The formal pool in this tranquil, shady garden reflects the sky and trees above. Right, *A sundial is the centrepeice of a sunny garden bed filled with lilies, miniature roses, coral bells and artemesia.*

MORE ON LIGHT:
THE SUNNY SIDE OF THE STREET

Light is a requirement of all flowering plants so few gardeners would complain that full or afternoon sun presents a problem. The difficulty arises when there is full sun and very dry soil (drought), or when there is not enough shade to offer some protection.

If there's too much sun in your garden, the best solution is to start planting trees. While they grow, try:

- Building a pergola or gazebo: A pergola is a three-dimensional structure made from wood or iron that originally evolved as a framework for growing wisteria, climbing roses and clematis. It not only gives shade, but it helps to define a special area for sitting or eating and offers privacy from buildings overlooking the garden.

- Adding a sun umbrella or awning: Garden umbrellas are handy for tables and small seating areas. For large spaces, a waterproof retractable awning provides an expanse of shade, cooling the house and tempering the drying effect of sun on containers. And in the event of an unforeseen shower on a planned outdoor dinner, it provides a ready-made umbrella, big enough for all.

DROUGHT-TOLERANT PLANTS

If nature gives you a lemon, make lemonade. And if nature gives you too much sun and too little rain or irrigation water, create a landscape using drought-tolerant plants. In the gardening world, this is referred to as xeriscaping, from the Latin word xeros, meaning "dry."

Good xeriscape plants include shrubs like yucca, cotoneaster, pyracantha, rugosa rose, rose-of-sharon, bluebeard (Caryopteris), potentilla and devil's walking stick (Aralia). Drought-tolerant perennials include succulents such as sedum and sempervivum as well as yarrow, lavender, anthemis, baby's breath, deadnettle (Lamium), sea thrift (Armeria), gaillardia, penstemon and thyme. Heat-loving annuals include African daisy, cosmos, Dahlberg daisy, gazania, portulaca and strawflower.

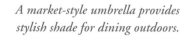

A market-style umbrella provides stylish shade for dining outdoors.

More on Light: The Shade Garden

Annabelle hydrangeas and ferns adapt well to the filtered light under trees.

S hade is a relative term for absence of sun, but most properties, unless hemmed in on all sides by tall buildings, get some sun.

Those that receive morning sun can grow all kinds of plants, usually ones described as preferring part sun or part shade. Woodland gardens, in which the spring sun warms the earth before the dense tree canopy leafs out, make ideal conditions for early bulbs and spring wildflowers, followed by summer shade-lovers.

Many gardens sit under a partial canopy of deciduous trees; this dappled light or moving shade supports plants recommended for light to moderate shade.

Hostas such as blue-gray 'Sieboldiana Elegans' are invaluable foliage plants for shady gardens.

DESIGN FOR SHADE GARDENS

Shade is often looked upon as a terrible drawback in a garden, but shady spaces can be quite magical — it's all in your point of view.

• Skillful pruning or selective removal of trees on densely shaded properties will increase the amount of sunshine reaching the garden.

• Create enchanting effects by your choice of plants. Ferns, hostas and other foliage plants are especially effective, as well as plants with variegated leaves. (Just don't mix too many variegated plants together or the result will be quite busy.)

• Move your seating areas, patio or other outdoor living spaces to a less shaded part of the garden.

A NEW SLANT ON SLOPES

Depending on the degree of grade, a slope can be a design nightmare or a chance to be creative. Gentle slopes can either be levelled or landscaped with lawn or plantings. But a steeper slope needs to be carefully planned to curb erosion and make it a useable part of the property. A rock garden can tame a slope while providing an opportunity to grow special plants that prefer sharp drainage. Terracing is effective, using low retaining walls of pressure-treated timber, reinforced concrete, brick or stone.

Higher masonry walls may be free-standing drystone (unmortared) or glued together with mortar. Drystone requires the wall to slant back into the slope slightly and a specific arrangement of the stones; mortared walls need a below-ground concrete footing. For these reasons, it's a good idea to do lots of research or get professional help if you plan to stack anything higher than a few layers of rock to retain soil.

Steep slopes can also create serious drainage problems at the foot of the slope. This damp area, which receives snowmelt in winter and rain in spring and fall, is a place loved by mosquitoes and hated by gardeners. Weeping tiles and gravel drainage go a long way to solving the problem but look to the plant world for a helping hand.

Design a bog garden using moisture-loving plants that demand the damp conditions other plants dislike. Try marsh marigolds and candelabra primroses for spring colour; royal ferns, Japanese iris, summersweet, ligularia and astilbe provide summer blooms, and for fall colour, heleniums, obedient plant, turtlehead and swamp mallow.

DESIGN FOR STEEP SLOPES

A steep slope, especially on a large property, may need landscaping with groundcovers and shrubs that spread quickly to curb erosion. Good choices include cotoneaster, juniper, periwinkle, bearberry, daylilies, hostas and rugged ornamental grasses. On large properties, rather than attempting to maintain a hillside in a conventional way, consider naturalizing it by interspersing wildflowers among long native grasses and shrubs.

This steep slope has a variety of plants that both add to the beauty of the garden while also preventing erosion.

SOIL

It pays to know your soil, because it has a huge bearing on the types of plants you can grow successfully in your garden. (For a comprehensive discussion on soil, see *Care* in this series.) Soil may be rich or poor, light to heavy, acid or alkaline. Luckily, most of these characteristics are not too difficult to change. Poor soils can be improved with garden compost, composted manures or other organic fertilizers. Those that are too porous or too heavy can be improved by forking in moisture-holding amendments like compost, leaf mould, peat moss and other bulky organic materials.

Knowing the composition of your soil before you plan will save time, money and energy in the long run.

MAGIC IN A JAR

Five Easy Steps to Analyzing Your Soil

A homemade test to find out the composition of your soil involves nothing more than a glass jar with its lid, some water, and a scoop or two of soil from your garden.

1. Fill the glass jar with water.
2. Add a scoop or two of garden soil — samples from different parts of the garden should not be mixed together.
3. Put the lid on the jar and shake it.
4. Let it sit for at least 24 hours.
5. Analyze the contents.

The soil will have settled into layers: sand on the bottom, then silt, clay, water, and organic matter floating on top.

If the sand, silt, and clay have settled into roughly equal proportions, and there is lots of organic material, you have good soil.

Soil high in clay will take longer to settle and the water can remain cloudy for more than a day.

Knowing the composition of your soil will help you determine what amendments might be required to help lawn and garden plants thrive.

SIZE AND SHAPE

A property that's big and square might not seem like a design problem, but it can create just as many difficulties for the designer as a garden that's small and narrow. No matter what you've got, you can make the most of it.

- Round off the corners of a square or rectangular yard with curved beds to make the garden more intimate. Use mass plantings of shrubs in these beds to fill up space.

- Divide a large yard into garden "rooms" by using shrubs, arbours and trellis for the "walls."

- A long narrow property can be divided into two areas — one close to the house, one farther away — to give the impression of a larger garden or emphasize its shape by running a handsome path down its length and planting on either side.

- Make a small garden look bigger with mass plantings — a single group of ferns or astilbe or lady's mantle will make the area look bigger than planting all three together in the same space.

- Use island beds to divide play areas from resting spots.

- Build in some hidden surprises; don't let the eye catch the whole garden at first glance.

The long, narrow shape of this pretty garden has been emphasized with a winding flagstone path planted with cushions of aromatic thyme.

DESIGNING A FLOWER BED

For a flower bed that's going to have maximum impact:

- Make all your flower beds bigger than you think they should be; many beginners make their beds too small.

- Don't be afraid to go back and increase the size of the bed once it's been planted and the plants seem to be getting too big for the space.

- Experiment with the shape; straight lines are not usually best.

- A cottage-style garden is produced by using curves and expansive borders.

- No matter the size or shape, use a rope or hose to mark out the flower beds before you dig and imagine the end result!

SMALL CAN BE JUST PERFECT

In this front yard, a simple planting scheme achieves balance and harmony in a small bed. The tree anchors the design; its height is perfectly proportioned to the width of the bed. The clipped boxwood shrubs provide a change in height, colour and texture. They have been placed far enough apart for flowers to be planted between them: in this case, red impatiens provide a classic contrast. Finally, the white sweet alyssum emphasizes the curved shape of the bed and neatly concludes the space between flowers and edge.

SCALE AND PROPORTION

Whether you're landscaping a tiny garden or a country estate, certain factors will influence the success of your design.

SCALE

Scale is the relationship in size between your house and garden elements, including plants. A huge house fronted with a pair of dwarf euonymus standards or a small bungalow obscured by a massive saucer magnolia each displays a poor sense of scale. Knowing the mature size of the trees, shrubs and other plant materials in your design will help you to master scale.

PROPORTION

Proportion is how you divide your property into usable space so the individual parts contribute to the success of the whole. Whether large and square, long and narrow or small as a backyard deck, good proportion means making the most of what you've got, and making sure the elements flow smoothly.

Thinking about your garden as a "house" and the areas in it as a series of "rooms" not only helps you sort out the different uses you have to make of the garden space, it also allows you to divide the garden by purpose. Then, the garden can be discovered slowly, rather than all at once, and can heighten interest in what's just out of sight. Remember, though, that indoor and outdoor proportions are very different, so make your defined garden areas bigger than you would if they were indoors.

DESIGN TIP

If you're new to gardening, start off with something small and aim to make it exquisite. You could start with a planting bed or a pair of matching terra cotta pots to place at your front door. You'll find getting started a rewarding experience that will teach you plenty. Then you'll be ready for more!

VIEWS

There are two kinds of garden views: those you want and those you don't!

But, much more than that, there are the views in your garden and those that go beyond your own yard. In Japanese landscape design, there's a phrase that translates as "borrowed scenery." It describes how one's own garden can be designed around a view across the fence—or across the city.

If you have a view you want to make the most of—whether it's in your garden or your neighbours'—frame it with trees and shrubs. Make sure you choose ones that won't grow too high or spread so much that eventually they will block the view you're trying to take advantage of.

But think carefully about the long-term impact of designing around a view outside your own property line. You never know when that view might change and you find yourself stuck with a garden designed around no view or something you'd rather not see at all.

If your challenge is to hide something unsightly that's within your own "four walls," you've got a number of options from which to choose.

Perhaps you can just eliminate the problem. Maybe it's time to replace that run-down garage with a small, neat tool shed. Or it might benefit from a paint job and some windowboxes overflowing with lobelia. An empty expanse of wall fronting on the garden can be beautified with the addition of trellises, a wall fountain or trompe-l'oeil painting technique.

If it's complete hiding you need, privacy lattice, dense screenings of shrubs or hedging plants and climbers are excellent choices. You can also try to deflect attention by creating a beautiful focal point, such as a fountain or rose-covered arbour, in another part of the garden.

The tall, vine-clad fence is a great backdrop for the garden plantings while providing privacy and hiding unsightly views.

OUT OF SIGHT, OUT OF MIND

Love having that barbecue and all your tools close to the back door, but hate looking at them? Plant shrubs to hid your storage area, or use inexpensive trellis, a little wood framing and a melange of potted plants to disguise necessities. Try the same approach to hide the garbage can, composter or heat exchanger.

GARDEN SHEDS AND STORAGE AREAS

There are all kinds of ways to stash the tools and hide the lawn mower. The garage works, of course — even if the car does end up outside. Aluminum sheds are inexpensive; place them on a concrete pad for longer wear. But if you want to turn a mere storage shed into haute design, consider giving it a cottage face and dressing it up with a pretty window and door.

Proof positive that a storage shed can be too pretty to be hidden away. Right, A garden shed can be a charming and integral part of the garden.

THINKING ABOUT STYLE

Although garden style depends to a large extent on personal taste, some architectural styles suit a certain look.

FORMAL HOUSE AND GARDEN STYLE

A formal house is usually defined by a sense of symmetry and balance and the landscape surrounding it typically conveys the same feeling. Formal design uses strong axial lines that move from the house to a major focal point, thereby "leading the eye" through the garden.

Formal style is distinguished by:

- sidewalks, walls and terraces often built with the same stone or brick used in the house
- geometric lines and shapes, in both the lawn and planting beds
- tightly pruned shrubs or topiaries
- a plant palette generally restricted to plants that perform dependably all season

INFORMAL HOUSE AND GARDEN STYLE

Many homes have an informal look that invites a relaxed approach to garden style. Here you find:

- curved walkways and free-form planting beds
- garden furnishings made from diverse materials including wood and modern synthetics
- a plant palette that encompasses a large and often eclectic collection of favourites—including vegetables, herbs and berries!

EVERY GARDEN SHOULD
REFLECT THE GARDENER

What makes a garden work? There's no magic formula. Part of it, of course, is good design; part is the skillful use of beautiful plants to create a certain effect.

But the intangible that makes each garden truly special is the "you" factor. What unmistakable signs of "you" will visitors find when walking through?

Formal garden style typically conveys a sense of symmetry and balance that mirrors the formal architecture of the house.

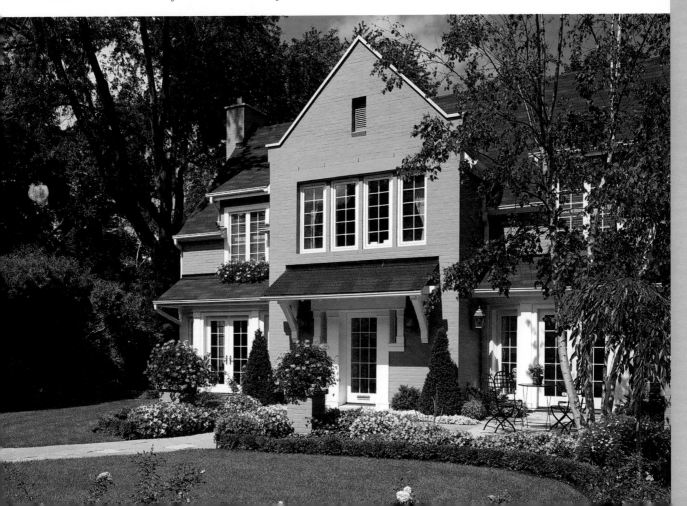

STYLED FOR COMFORTABLE LIVING

A garden like this, with its raised decks and ample, comfy furnishings becomes an extension of the house, providing another "room" for gracious entertaining.

SPECIAL STYLE: THE JAPANESE GARDEN

Many people love the serenity of the Japanese garden with its three elements: water, plants and stone. Colour is subdued, apart from the green of foliage plants and the grey of stone or aged wood. Whether a raked-gravel Zen garden or merely a stone pagoda set in an evocative and textural planting, Japanese-inspired principles are easy to adopt, either in whole to create an entire landscape, or, in part, to incorporate a small vignette.

In Japanese landscapes, use of stone lanterns such as this moss-encrusted pedestal lantern originated with the tea gardens of the 15th and 16th centuries.

FINDING THE FOCUS

You walk into a garden and your eyes are immediately drawn to "it." To what? To that fountain, statue, collection of bird houses, wooden bench . . . you get the idea. Every garden needs one large design element that states categorically: "This place was built around me." We call these attention-getters focal points.

A focal point should be intriguing, capturing the interest of those who enter the garden — much like a beautiful painting or piece of furniture attracts the attention of visitors inside your home.

There is no end to the types of focal points you can choose according to your garden style. Here are some suggestions to help get your creative juices flowing:

In the formal garden:

- formal statuary
- cast iron urns used as planters placed on either side of the front door
- an Italian fountain
- a regal three-tiered bird bath
- sculpted shrubs or a piece of topiary

In the informal garden:

- a rose arbour or even more casual, a twig arbour
- a sundial
- a white picket fence and gate
- a water garden

A stone bust rests on the seat of a charming birch-bark arbour, creating an unusual focal point in this lush shade garden. Right, Roses form a soft, delicate backdrop to the sundial for a focal point with a romantic touch.

In the small garden:

- a bird bath
- a small fountain
- a trellis or obelisk supporting a beautiful climbing plant

On the deck or patio:

- big containers overflowing with beautifully tended flowers
- bird houses and feeders
- wooden or iron sculpture

DESIGN TIPS

In the new garden, try any of these ideas to create a focal point:
- a variety of containers, carefully planted and meticulously maintained
- an obelisk in a container, to create vertical interest
- a huge sun umbrella
- an interesting choice for a shed, complete with windowboxes

Left, *A lovely garden statue is surrounded by low growing plants to further emphasize its use as a focal point in the garden. Right, A stone path leads to a pretty arch festooned with yellow roses. By placing the arch at the end of the path, the designer has made it a focal point while creating a pleasant transition from path to lawn.*

FOCAL POINT DESIGN: CONTAINERS

Strong focal points can be created by using containers, either overflowing with plants or left to stand empty. Stunning containers such as classical urns make wonderful design features and focal points. Set at the end of a path, the urn will attract the eye and draw the visitor into the garden.

In a small garden, one bold container will be more dramatic than a group of small ones fighting for space. But where space is not a problem, a group of containers will be more impressive and less likely to be lost than a single container. Using a container as a focal point makes the container and its plants the star. For this reason, both the container and its plants should be carefully chosen, and the plants tended daily to keep them looking their best.

Containers can be especially useful in adding height into a garden. On the deck or patio, a beautiful wrought-iron or wooden obelisk in a planter can support a flowering vine or clematis. In the flower bed, an inverted pot can form the support for a container placed on top. Used this way, the container will introduce height, colour and interest into the garden.

DESIGN TIP

A container on a tall pedestal makes a strong statement and is best used in a more formal garden. However, if you want to place such a container in a slightly less formal setting, soften it with ivy tumbling out. Set against a hedge or in a corner, it will add life to a drab space.

An urn tucked away in the garden is a pretty focal point while contributing height to the flower bed. Right, Bright containers marching up the steps bring colour up and off the ground.

FOCAL POINT DESIGN: WATER

Water enhances any garden: large, small, formal, informal, urban, suburban or rural. Even as a simple bird bath, water can be a powerful focal point.

Still water, such as that in a pond, water garden or swimming pool, offers a marvelous reflective quality, displaying the mirror-image of the plants and garden features that surround it.

Moving water, such as in a fountain or waterfall, is stimulating to the eye while creating an air of tranquillity. The sound of trickling or bubbling water is immensely soothing to the soul. In our modern urban environments, it provides a genuine benefit in the form of white noise to help block out the constant drone of cars, trucks, planes and people.

A garden pond with fish, water lilies and the sound of gently splashing water creates a strong focus in the garden.

SWIMMING POOLS

A swimming pool is a focal point that dominates the landscape. The first and primary concern about pools is safety. Here are some ideas to beautify the pool in your garden, while ensuring that whatever you add to the pool surround doesn't create obstacles that could cause kids or adults to take a tumble.

Lush ornamental grasses planted in pockets of the stone surround of this pool have created a natural, lagoon-like effect.

- If you're planning a pool, think long and hard about where it should be situated. Also think about the effect created by different shapes and sizes, and different coloured liners in vinyl pools or paint in concrete pools. A black liner in a freeform-shaped pool with a flagstone deck is a very sophisticated look. If you want a pool that's playful and practical, you may opt for a more traditionally coloured blue or turquoise liner or paint. Also, think about how it will look in the winter; if you don't care for the closed-up appearance, locate the pool farther from the house or slightly hide it from view.

- If your pool is blue, teal or turquoise, use that same colour in furnishings such as cushion covers or sun umbrellas. Build your plant colour scheme around these colours. (See Getting Creative with Colour, page 52.)

- Consider sculpting pockets from the paving around the pool to plant with lush ornamental grasses.

- Containers are a perfect answer to planting around the pool. They can be moved to the pool's edge for quiet moments when you want to use the water's surface to reflect the containers and plants or taken away for active swimming times.

MAKING AN ENTRANCE

Althought it may not be where you spend the most time, the front garden:

- is the first impression your home conveys to the neighbourhood
- softens the architecture of your house and connects it to the street
- is a place to grow favourite plants, especially when sunshine creates better growing conditions there than in the back yard
- is the entrance hall through which the world beats a path to your front door

A front yard must satisfy certain physical needs, including transporting to the front door everyone from the new baby in the stroller to the appliance delivery man. Here are other important points about the front garden:

- Accessibility: don't crowd the front door area with containers or overgrown shrubs. There should be a place where people can stand before they enter the house.

- Functionality: for instance, think about where the mail box will be placed, so the mail carrier doesn't beat a hasty, daily exit through your rose bed.

- Security: don't plan for shrubs or large trees that obscure the view of the front door from the street. Make sure the entryway and front path are well lit.

DESIGN TIP

Many front gardens conform to a traditional recipe. Lots of lawn, a sidewalk leading from the driveway or street, a tree or two and an assortment of foundation plants against the house. Much wonderful gardening space is left untouched in such a plan.

Apply the same thinking to the front yard as you would to the back. Consider the bones — the underlying structure — of this garden space and build on them with planting beds, focal points, furnishings and plants. The front garden is a wonderful opportunity to show off your gardening skills and distinguish your house in the neighbourhood.

An arched gate and garden starting right at the street create a sense of welcome and maximize the space available for planting.

GARDEN GATES

Gates do more than merely usher us in: they can make the entrance to the back garden an anticipated event. Gates offer security, create a sense of sanctuary, extend the architectural theme of the house right to the street and provide a framework for climbing roses and twining vines. They can sport arches overhead or feature ornamental "see-through" grates that give visitors a sneak preview of the garden beyond.

This charming, old wrought iron gate offers a sense of enclosure while giving passersby a view into the romantic front garden. Right, A simple path made from flagstones set flush in the lawn leads the visitor into a series of garden rooms in this long, narrow garden.

PATHS TO PERFECTION

Perfect paths are the crowning touch to making a grand entrance to the garden, front or back. There's a wide variety of building materials to use — from the decorative type of path created by laying a mosaic, to the practical choice of concrete pavers. The choice is up to you and the garden style you are creating.

DESIGNING A WALKWAY

• Although paths and walkways in the back garden can be any dimension and material that suits your plan, the sidewalk to the front door should be generous in width — no narrower than 1.3 m (4 feet).

• Whether poured concrete, precast concrete paving slabs, random or regular cut flagstone or interlock pavers, the front walk should be smooth, flat and built on a well-compacted foundation.

• Soften the look of a walk with plantings on one or both sides and make it safe with path lighting.

• Gradually widen or flare the walk as it approaches the front landing or porch stairs.

• It's a great idea to make your walkway flush with the lawn so that you can run the mower right over the walkway and save yourself lots of trimming.

PLANTS AND DESIGN

Garden plants could fill a whole book—so that's exactly what we did. We filled a whole book, *Plantings*, with fabulous ideas for designing with trees, shrubs and flowers. These pages, though, will give you the basics for designing with plants.

TREES: For providing the backbone of the garden or as decorative features, trees are unsurpassed. Just consider all that trees bring to a garden: shade; privacy; colour through their bark, branches, blossoms, leaves and berries; shape that can be naturally conical, round, weeping, tall, thin, wide or pruned to your choice; winter interest; and patterns of light and shadow.

Trees deserve a place in every garden. When you're choosing a tree, give it enough room to show off its natural beauty.

SHRUBS: Another family of plants that makes a huge contribution to good garden bones, shrubs can provide screening, seasonal variety, colour, scent and shape. Consider both coniferous and deciduous varieties and position them according to their mature size and the time of year they are at their best. A colourful fall shrub such as witch hazel may be better farther from the house so it can be viewed as a bright spot in the garden, whereas one with delicate flowers, such as mountain laurel, is better closer to the house where it's more easily seen.

PERENNIALS: Perennials give the gardener a chance to experiment with form, texture, colour, size and shape. There's an almost endless variety from which to choose. Plant them in blocks of colour, and then enjoy them year after year.

ANNUALS: The blooming workhorse of the garden, annuals are a must for the nonstop colour they deliver. In the early days of a new garden, annuals can fill in spots while young perennials and shrubs are getting established. In containers, they dress up decks and neglected corners.

BULBS: The spectacular variety of colours that bulbs deliver means that they should be planted where they can be seen and enjoyed. They're essential in the front garden, and think, too, of how they could brighten your back yard view.

Every garden needs a variety of plants, including trees, shrubs, perennials-such as purple coneflower and heliopsis in the foreground-annuals and bulbs.

49

MORE ON PLANTS

SEQUENCE OF PLANTING: Large plants go at the back of the flowerbed, mid-sized plants in the middle and short plants at the front.

TEXTURE: Plants with small, delicate flowers are best appreciated close to where you sit or walk, so put them along a path, at the front of a border or in a container on a deck, stairs or patio.

Plants with bold dramatic leaves can overwhelm other plants, especially in a small garden. Situate them where they can shine on their own.

The texture of a leaf or petal also affects the way we perceive its colour. A ridged leaf looks a different shade of green than a smooth, shiny one.

Texture can refer not only to the individual leaf or petal, but to the impression the plant makes. A group of tiny white flowerheads, such as those on baby's breath, has a different texture than the white of a mass of daisies.

VARIETY: Every garden needs a variety of plants chosen for their habit (shape of plant), shape of leaf, colour and height. Height ranges from trees to groundcovers, which includes the lawn. While trees are growing, introduce height in the garden by growing vines and climbing plants on fences or walls, or by using obelisks in containers.

USE OF SPACE: Forget the idea that you have to squeeze your plantings to the edge of your yard and save the middle expanse for lawn. Use all your property to design your garden, just the way a painter uses the entire canvas. When you "paint" your garden masterpiece, plan for line, form and harmonious blocks of flower and foliage colour in your garden.

DESIGN TIP

Assess the "visual weight" of plant masses, especially in asymmetrical groupings. For instance, a tall slender group of plants is balanced by a lower growing mound.

Plants need to be chosen for their shape, height, texture and colour. Flowers are transient but foliage must perform all season long.

GETTING CREATIVE WITH COLOUR

Colour works in magical or mysterious ways, warming up a garden or cooling it down, capturing the observer's attention or adding an element of sophistication. Because colour has a strong effect, it's wise to know how to use it effectively.

The colour wheel is a system for organizing the colour spectrum and is extremely helpful when you think about colour. The basis of the wheel is the primary colours: red, yellow and blue. By adding half of one primary colour to half of another primary colour, secondary colours are created: green, violet and orange. Finally, intermediate colours are created by mixing adjacent primary and secondary colours equally. So by mixing red with orange, an orange-red colour is achieved. The colour wheel shows which colours complement, harmonize or contrast with each other.

Complementary colour schemes are a pleasing combination of colours that use colours opposite each other on the colour wheel. For example, yellow and violet are complementary.

Harmonious colours produce the effect their name would suggest: one of peace and harmony. It is achieved by using colours that are beside each other on the colour wheel, such as blue, blue-violet and violet.

Contrasting colours are based on the contrasting pairs of red-green, blue-orange, and yellow-purple. This colour scheme can produce a bold statement in the garden, and is especially difficult to produce successfully in planting beds.

DESIGN TIP

Effective use of colour hinges on selecting colours which complement, harmonize or contrast with each other. So where do you start? Pick the colour you like best, in a single plant or group of plants, or even your favourite porch rocker, and use that as your first building block. Decide if you want a colour scheme that is vibrant and lively (use a contrasting colour palette), a less pronounced colour statement (a complementary scheme) or a calm, restful combination (harmonious colours).

A burst of seasonal colour in a large container can perk up the entryway when garden flowers are past their prime.

DESIGNING WITH COLOUR

There is also a lot of discussion these days about monochromatic gardens—those composed of just one colour. The only true monochromatic garden is the all-green garden, created by mixing non-flowering plants. Other so-called monochromatic schemes such as the all-white garden are, in fact, a mix of white flowers with green foliage. The gardener creating the monochromatic garden must be keenly aware of the use of texture, leaf shapes and sizes, and lighting: monochromatic gardens are a challenge!

The green in this bed effectively separates the colours of the flowers and provides an important visual "break."

COLOUR: WHITE

White flowers can be used to lighten or break up other colour schemes. Because they have greater visibility in low light, white flowers and variegated plants are popular with gardeners who work during the day and want to enjoy their garden in the evening or at night.

COLOUR: BLUE

Plants with blue or purple flowers or with blue-grey foliage create a restful feeling. Use them to create a misty, ethereal effect. Blue flowers also pair beautifully with yellow flowers; the two colours are classically complementary.

COLOUR: PINK

Pink-flowered plants and those with wine-coloured foliage create a warm, pleasing effect. Punch up pastel schemes with more intense pinks. Pink flowers look lovely with silver foliage plants.

THE SEASONS OF A GARDEN

A well-designed garden is a joy in all seasons. Reap the rewards each season delivers . . .

SPRING — Use bulbs, flowering shrubs, bleeding heart, pansies and a cloud of forget-me-nots to herald spring's return to the garden. The vibrant colours of spring flowers can brighten the path to your front door after the long winter.

SUMMER — The flower garden is at its glory and warm days and nights invite you to spend every possible moment outdoors. Concentrate your growing efforts near your outdoor living spaces: patios, decks, porches and swimming pools.

AUTUMN — When summer's blooms fade, turn to fall foliage and annuals to lend colour to the garden. Dwarf burning bush (*Euonymous alatus* 'Compactus') turns a brilliant carmine-pink or serviceberry (Amelanchier) becomes a mottled red and orange. Annuals, like chrysanthemums or ornamental cabbage, can be placed around the garden in containers to add life and colour.

WINTER — The "bones" of the garden are laid bare; good bones do the garden and its designer proud. A carefully composed selection of conifers may appear uniform in summer, but, through the haze of a frosty winter morning, the striking silhouettes, the variations in height and shape and the gentle gradations of grey and green with red berries and branches provide a welcome change from the fluffy blanket of snow.

FIVE WAYS TO CREATE A GREAT GARDEN DESIGN

1. START

This sounds obvious but a lot of the best learning about a garden is done by trial and error. Remember, there's very little of what you plant in a garden that is absolutely permanent. If there's something you don't like replace the offending plant, or move it, but just get started, and then keep trying.

2. DON'T DO TOO MUCH WHEN YOU'RE JUST STARTING

Gardening is a science, a hobby — and an art. You'll be happier with the results if you start gradually, learn as you go and work your way up to bigger things.

3. BE METHODICAL

There is a process which should be followed in the design of a garden. It goes like this: big jobs first. It can be frustrating to spend time making a lovely flower bed by your back patio only to see it flattened by the construction of a new deck. Build beds where you can be reasonably confident the plants will have a chance to grow and develop. If there's a chance that new construction will be undertaken, satisfy your immediate urge to garden by planting in containers.

4. PLANT A TREE

Trees make one of the single greatest contributions to beautiful gardens. Don't overlook these beauties as you rush to plant flowers.

5. MAKE A PLAN

A good garden is a planned garden; a good gardener is a gardener with an action plan no matter how large or small. Here's a review of what your action plan should include:

- Where you want to begin: front yard or back?

- What you're trying to accomplish with your garden: functionality (a garden that produces flowers for cutting, fruits, vegetables, herbs?), beauty or a combination of both?

- A clear definition of the garden style you feel most comfortable with — formal, informal, cottage, Japanese?

- What you will use for a focal point, or points, and where it, or they, will be located?

- A list of all construction jobs for the short and long term.

- What garden rooms you want to create, and where: living? dining? playroom?

- The plants you want to include, selected for their growing requirements and what you like.

- A time frame: do you plan to live in this home for a lifetime or do you see a move in the not-too-distant future? This can have a great impact on what you will be prepared to put into the garden.

A swimming pool can be integrated into the garden with adjacent planting beds featuring soft, romantic plantings.

INDEX

ISBN: 0-9697259-3-0

Produced for Loblaws Inc. by Alpha Corporation/Susan Yates, Publisher
Written for Loblaws Inc. by Ted Johnston and Janet Davis
Landscape design consultant and horticultural expert: Janet Rosenberg
Photographs and horticultural editing: Janet Davis
Photographs by Sharon Kish: cover, p. 3, 4, 5, 13, 14, 17, 19, 21, 23, 25, 29, 30, 31, 33, 34, 37, 38, 40, 41, 42, 45, 49, 53, 54, 55, 57, 58, 59, 60, 61, 63, inside back cover
Copy editor: Greg Iaonnou/Colborne Communications
Text and cover design: Dave Murphy/ArtPlus Ltd.
Page layout: Leanne Knox/ArtPlus Ltd.
Printed and bound in Canada by Kromar Printing

GARDEN DESIGN CREDITS

p. 6 Judith Kennedy; p. 15 Zora Buchanan; p. 18 Laura Grant; p. 24 Anderson Garden Services; p. 26 Derek Bennett; p. 35 Butchart Gardens; p. 36 Horticultural Design; p. 43 Gary Koller; p. 46 Pam Chorley; p. 47 Derek Bennett; p. 56 Judith Kennedy; Janet Rosenberg & Associates: p. 3, 4, 5, 9, 10, 11, 13, 14, 17, 19, 21, 23, 25, 29, 30, 31, 33, 34, 37, 38, 39, 41, 45, 55, 57, 59, 60, 61, 63, inside back cover